Grab a Life Jacket, SCOOBY-DOO!

A Guide to WATER SAFETY

by Steve Korté

PEBBLE
a capstone imprint

Published by Pebble, an imprint of Capstone
1710 Roe Crest Drive, North Mankato, Minnesota 56003
capstonepub.com

Copyright © 2025 Hanna-Barbera.
SCOOBY-DOO and all related characters and elements are trademarks of and © Hanna-Barbera. (s25)

All rights reserved. No part of this publication may be reproduced in whole or in part, or stored in a retrieval system, or transmitted in any form or by any means, electronic, mechanical, photocopying, recording, or otherwise, without written permission of the publisher.

Library of Congress Cataloging-in-Publication Data
Names: Korté, Steve, author. Title: Grab a life jacket, Scooby-Doo! : a guide to water safety / by Steve Korté. Description: North Mankato, Minnesota : Pebble, [2025] | Series: Scooby-doo's dos and don'ts | Audience: Ages 5-8 | Audience: Grades 2-3 | Summary: "When it's hot outside, kids often want to cool off by going swimming. Before they go, Scooby-Doo and friends have a list of water safety rules. From wearing sunscreen and listening to lifeguards to watching the weather, kids who follow these basic safety tips will have the most fun in the sun!"—Provided by publisher. Identifiers: LCCN 2024056003 (print) | LCCN 2024056004 (ebook) | ISBN 9798875220753 (hardcover) | ISBN 9798875220708 (paperback) | ISBN 9798875220715 (pdf) | ISBN 9798875220722 (epub) | ISBN 9798875220739 (kindle edition) Subjects: LCSH: Aquatic sports—Safety measures—Juvenile literature. | Scooby-Doo (Fictitious character)—Juvenile literature. Classification: LCC GV770.6 .K67 2025 (print) | LCC GV770.6 (ebook) | DDC 797.20028/9—dc23/eng/20250113
LC record available at https://lccn.loc.gov/2024056003
LC ebook record available at https://lccn.loc.gov/2024056004

Image Credits
Capstone: Bobbie Nuytten (stop sign), 16 (top), 30, 32; Getty Images: AaronAmat, 25, aire images, 10, Andrei Savin, 5, angela auclair, 8, artisteer, 15, BestVector, 2 (bottom) and throughout, Cavan Images, 26, Chadchai Krisadapong, 21, Chris Dela Cruz, 12, Erik Isakson, 18, gchutka, 14, goldenKB, 22, Jose Luis Pelaez Inc, 6, Rubberball/Erik Isakson, 13, SerrNovik, 4, the_burtons, 16 (bottom), Westend61, 20, zeljkosantrac, 24; Shutterstock: AnEduard, 27, Bernardo Emanuelle, 28, ClaireWilliamsArt, 11, Jessica2, 7, Max Topchii, cover, Nataliya Turpitko, 17, Polina Tomtosova (doodles), 1 and throughout, watercolor 15 (notepad), back cover and throughout, Yuricazac, 9

Editorial Credits
Editor: Christianne Jones; Designer: Bobbie Nuytten; Media Researcher: Svetlana Zhurkin; Production Specialist: Katy LaVigne

Printed and bound in China. 6274

Scooby-Doo and the Mystery Inc. gang work hard to keep everyone safe from ghosts and villains. On a rare day off, they like to spend time at the beach. But there are a lot of dangers around water. Water safety means keeping yourself and others safe when you are in or near water. When you don't know what to do, just ask Scooby-Doo!

It's a beautiful summer day. The sun is shining. I'm ready to go swimming, but I forgot to put on sunscreen. My friends are already in the water.

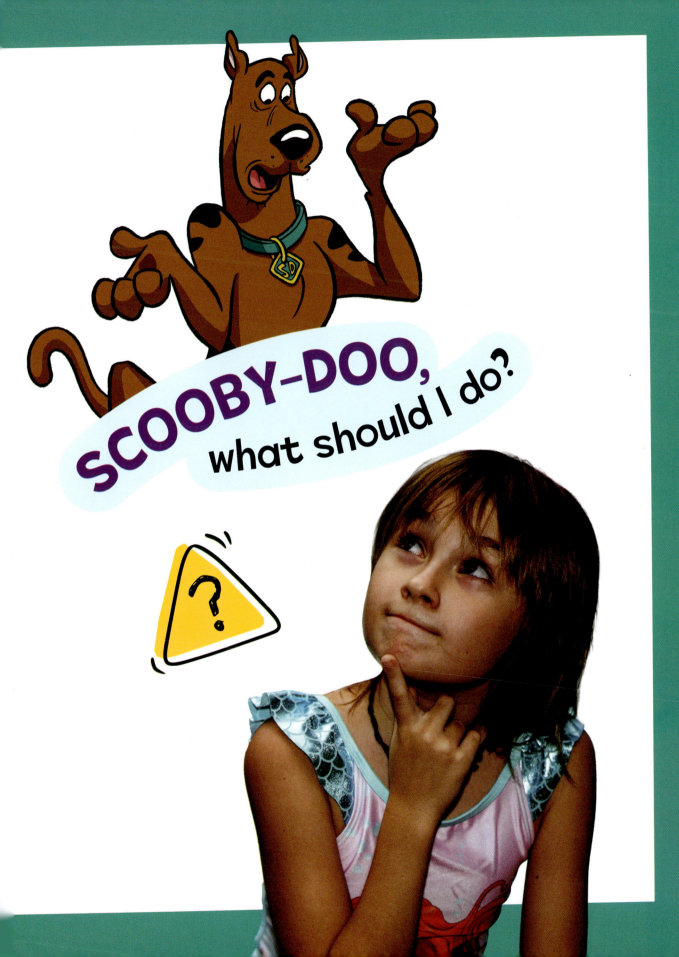

Stop and put on sunscreen! It protects your skin from burns and keeps you safe under the sun. Be sure to reapply too.

When you swim, the sun's harmful UV rays reflect off the surface of the water. The parts of your body above the water will burn faster.

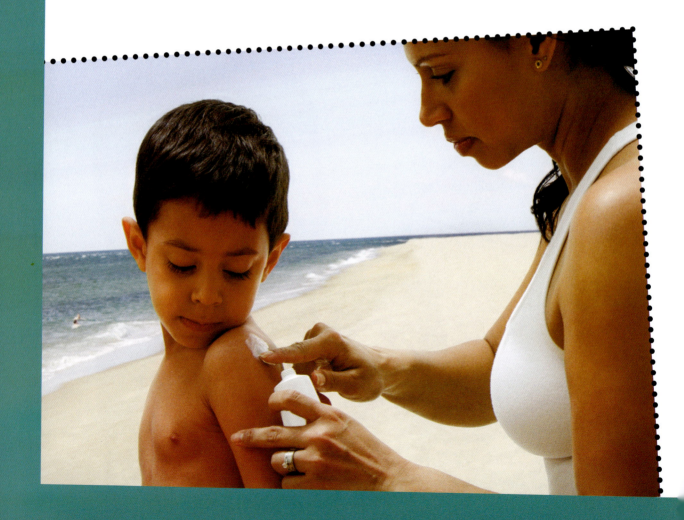

DON'T FORGET!

Even on a cloudy day, the sun's rays can burn you.

Shaggy's Sunscreen Safety Tips

- Use a sunscreen with an SPF of 30 or higher.
- Don't use sunscreen if the expiration date has passed.
- Apply sunscreen at least 15 minutes before heading outside.
- Reapply sunscreen every two hours and after swimming.

My friends and I are having a great time at the pool. But then the clouds roll in. *Ka-boom!* Is that thunder?

Swimming during bad weather is very dangerous. If you hear thunder or see lightning, you need to get out of the water right away. You should find a safe place indoors.

My friends and I are excited for our beach day. We are ready to swim, but the lifeguard isn't on duty yet.

You should wait for the lifeguard. Lifeguards are trained to keep everyone safe. If someone is in trouble, they know how to rescue them. They enforce water safety rules so a day at the beach can be fun and safe.

Fred's Beach Safety Rules

- Only swim at beaches with a lifeguard on duty.
- Always swim with a buddy.
- Only swim in the marked swim areas.
- Always jump into the water feet first.

Why did Scooby-Doo wear a snorkel to the beach?

He wanted to go "Scooby-Diving!"

I just learned how to dive, and I really want to show my friends. The dock is long, but I don't know how deep the water is at the end.

Diving can be dangerous, especially if you can't see the bottom of where you are diving. You could hit your head.

Ask an adult if it's safe. Then jump feet first to test the water. Feel for rocks. Check how deep the water is. If it's safe, you can dive all day.

DON'T FORGET!

Water should be at least 9 feet deep for safe diving.

Where do ghosts like to go swimming?

The Dead Sea!

My best friend is swimming in the deep end of the pool. It looks really fun. I'm still learning to swim, but I want to swim together.

You should stay in the shallow end of the pool. Your friend can come and swim with you instead. Work at becoming a stronger swimmer with lessons and practice.

Daphne's Pool Safety Rules

- Walk on the pool deck because it can be slippery.
- Don't push or goof around in the water or on the pool deck.
- Listen to the lifeguards.
- Swim with a buddy.
- Know your limits.

What do you fill with water but it doesn't sink?

A swimming pool!

My family is spending the day on the river with some friends. We have enough kayaks, canoes, and floaties. But we don't have enough life jackets.

When you are on a boat, raft, tube, or swimming in open water, you should always wear a life jacket—even if you are an excellent swimmer.

DON'T FORGET!

Your life jacket should fit snug enough that you can't slip out of it, but it shouldn't be too tight either.

Scooby-Doo and the gang want you to have a fun and safe water experience. Just remember to follow a few simple and SAFE rules.

Swim with a buddy.

Always wear sunscreen.

Follow rules by the lifeguards.

Exit the water if you hear thunder or see lightning.

Scooby-Doo's
Water Safety Review

1. How often should you reapply sunscreen?
   a. every 10 minutes
   b. every 2 hours
   c. every 12 hours

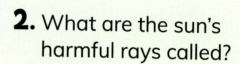

2. What are the sun's harmful rays called?
   a. UV
   b. AB
   c. XY

3. If you are swimming and hear thunder, where should you go?
   a. under a tree
   b. indoors
   c. under the water

4. Who is trained to keep you safe at the pool or beach?
   a. friends
   b. teachers
   c. lifeguards

5. When should you swim alone?
   a. on your birthday
   b. never
   c. whenever you want

6. How should a life jacket fit?
   a. a little loose
   b. snug
   c. as tight as possible

7. When should you wear a life jacket?
   a. on a boat
   b. at school
   c. in the car

8. How deep should water be for safe diving?
   a. 1 inch
   b. 4 feet
   c. 9 feet

ANSWERS: 1. b 2. a 3. b 4. c 5. b 6. b 7. a 8. c

How many signs can YOU find?

There are different warning signs throughout this book. See how many of each you can find!

About the Author

Steve Korté is the author of more than 100 books, featuring characters as diverse as Batman, Bigfoot, and the Loch Ness Monster. As a former editor at DC Comics, he worked on hundreds of titles, including 75 Years of DC Comics, Wonder Woman: The Complete History, and Jack Cole and Plastic Man. He lives in New York City with his husband Bill.